Nachshon, *Who Was* Afraid *to* Swim

A PASSOVER STORY

For my mother, Carol Bodin, who taught me to swim—D.B.C.

For my lovely wife, Alex, and the marvelous Lily Peach—J.

Pronunciation: The "ch" in Nachshon is pronounced like the "ch" in Bach.

KAR-BEN PUBLISHING INC.
A division of Lerner Publishing Group, Inc.
241 First Avenue North
Minneapolis, MN 55401
1-800-4KARBEN

Website address: www.karben.com

Library of Congress Cataloging-in-Publication Data

Cohen, Deborah Bodin, 1968—
   Nachshon who was afraid to swim: a passover story/by Deborah Bodin Cohen: illustrated by Jago
      p.   cm.
      Summary: When the Israelites flee Egypt, Nachshon exhibits great courage by being the first to step into the Red Sea, even though he cannot swim.
      ISBN 978-0-8225-8764-4 (lib. bdg. : alk. paper) [1. Slavery—
Fiction. 2. Courage—Fiction. 3. Fear—Fiction. 4. Bible stories—O.T. Exodus—Fiction.] I. Jago, ill. II Title.
      PZ7. c6623Nac 2009
   [E]—dc22   20070428359

Manufactured in the United States of America
1 2 3 4 5 6 – DP – 14 13 12 11 10 09

Nachshon, *Who Was* Afraid *to* Swim

A PASSOVER STORY

By Deborah Bodin Cohen

Illustrations by Jago

KAR-BEN
PUBLISHING

In the days when Pharaoh ruled and the pyramids cast their shadows over Egypt, there lived an Israelite slave named Nachshon. Nachshon's parents, grandparents, and even his great-great-grandparents had lived as slaves. But Nachshon knew that long ago his family had been free, and he dreamed of freedom every night.

From dawn to dusk, under the midday rays of the desert sun, Nachshon's father and brothers labored in the quarries mixing straw and mud into bricks.

Nachshon slipped past the taskmasters and smuggled in cool drinking water for them.

Neither the Egyptian taskmasters nor Pharaoh himself scared the young boy. His family began calling him "Brave Nachshon."

When Pharaoh and his royal courtiers arrived in the city market, most slaves fled in fear. Not Nachshon. He trailed behind and spied on them. Whatever Nachshon learned, he reported to the Israelite elders. Soon everyone began calling him "Brave Nachshon."

Nachshon, though, had one fear. In the evening, when most slaves took a cool swim in the River Nile, Nachshon stood anxiously on the river's edge. He put his toes in the water and trembled. Some days, he imagined a giant crocodile grabbing his legs. Other days, he pictured himself sinking slowly to the river's bottom, as though bricks were tied to his ankles. The other slaves began calling him "Brave Nachshon, who is afraid to swim."

When Nachshon grew old enough, the taskmasters demanded that he join his father and brothers in the quarries. Each day was long, dull, and dusty. The years passed slowly. As much as he dreamed of freedom, Nachshon feared he would always be a slave.

Just when Nachshon began to give up hope, a stranger arrived, promising freedom for the Israelites. News of the visitor spread like a sandstorm. Nachshon ran to the river bank to join the crowd waiting to hear him speak.

"His name is Moses," whispered a fellow slave. "He says he is an Israelite, but was raised in the royal palace until Pharaoh learned his true identity. Then he ran away. He says that God has sent him back to Egypt to demand our freedom."

Nachshon's heart leaped at the sight. Moses' face glowed like the sun and his eyes glistened like stars. He held a sapphire blue shepherd's staff, carved in the shape of a serpent. Though he spoke haltingly, his message was clear.

"You must have faith that freedom is possible," Moses proclaimed, holding his staff toward the heavens. "Real freedom means trusting in God. Real freedom means believing in yourself."

That evening, their hope renewed, the Israelite slaves played in the cool waters of the Nile. "Brave Nachshon, come celebrate with us," called his friends. "Even today, with the possibility of freedom, are you still afraid to swim?"

Moses saw Nachshon hesitate. He walked over, bent down, and whispered into the boy's ear. "Real freedom means facing your fears and overcoming them." Nachshon looked at the river and repeated Moses' words to himself. It took all his courage just to dangle his legs into the current and splash some water on his body.

The next morning, Moses approached Pharaoh and demanded freedom for the Israelites. Pharaoh's heart was hard. He not only rejected the plea, he made the Israelites work harder.

But Moses told the people not to give up hope. "God will send plagues over Egypt to soften Pharaoh's heart," he predicted.

When God sent locusts, Nachshon picked each and every insect off the few vegetables in his family's small garden.

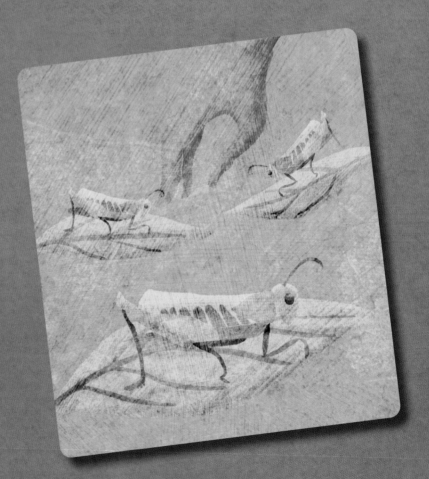

The plagues did not frighten Nachshon. When God sent frogs, Nachshon caught a pair in a basket and let his nephews and nieces play with them.

When God made the land pitch black, with light only in Israelite homes, Nachshon ventured outside to check on his neighbors.

Finally Pharaoh gave in. He told Moses to take the Israelites and leave. Nachshon and his family packed quickly, without time even to let their bread rise. The Israelites headed to the Sea of Reeds and camped on its shores.

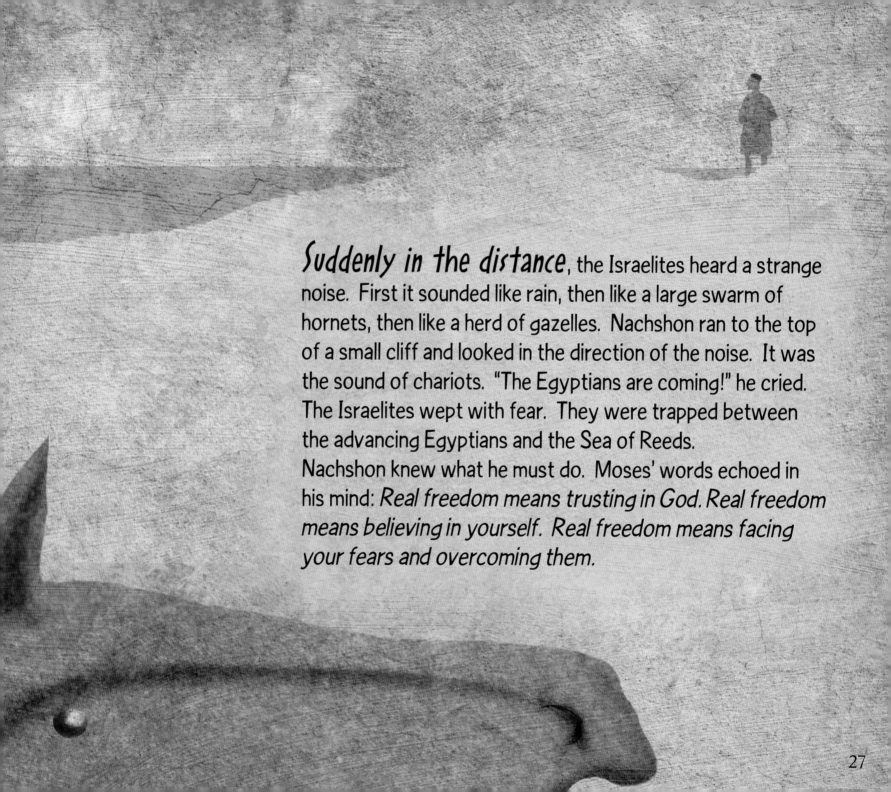

Suddenly in the distance, the Israelites heard a strange noise. First it sounded like rain, then like a large swarm of hornets, then like a herd of gazelles. Nachshon ran to the top of a small cliff and looked in the direction of the noise. It was the sound of chariots. "The Egyptians are coming!" he cried. The Israelites wept with fear. They were trapped between the advancing Egyptians and the Sea of Reeds.

Nachshon knew what he must do. Moses' words echoed in his mind: *Real freedom means trusting in God. Real freedom means believing in yourself. Real freedom means facing your fears and overcoming them.*

Nachshon stepped slowly into the sea. The water rose from his toes, to his ankles, to his knees, to his waist, to his shoulders, to his chin, to his lips. Nachshon repeated silently, "Face your fears, have faith." Just as the water was about to cover his head, a miracle occurred. Moses lifted his staff to the heavens and a strong east wind pushed back the water, creating a dry path through the sea.

All the Israelites joined Nachshon and walked with him to **freedom.**

When they reached the opposite shore, the Israelites broke into song.

But Nachshon simply waded in the sea and let the cool waters remind him that he was free. Free from slavery and free from his fears.

Author's Note

The Torah includes brief references to Nachshon ben Aminadav. He is a leader of the tribe of Judah. His sister Elisheva marries Aaron. In the Midrash or Rabbinic lore, Nachshon's story is more fully developed. He becomes an example of faith and courage. The rabbis imagine Nachshon as the first Israelite to step into the Sea of the Reeds. Only when water reaches Nachshon's nostrils does God part the sea.